Praise for *Bread from a* [barcode: T0151667]

"'I wanted my words to come closer th   o
Montale said, and added, 'closer to what?'   :e
come alive, but language encodes it. Montale yearned for 'the end of the il-
lusion of the world as representation.' Janlori Goldman's exquisite poems
enter a world which is immediate beyond rhetoric—'walnuts fall, still in
their shell's shell.' It's a place of visceral danger, on the cusp of vanishing it-
self, but the 'last month' is just before birth. Goldman's lines quicken with
the pulse of a singular life. The vision is intimate and the lyricism grounded.
'I'm as close to god as I'll ever come/or want to be,' Goldman writes; the sa-
cred is everywhere, but it's human, raw, confounding, a homeless stranger
who doesn't happen to be hungry, sleeping in a window well, 'her sneakers
on the sidewalk/like slippers by a bed.' *Bread from a Stranger's Oven* is a book
of stunning ambition and accomplishment." —D. Nurkse

"Through her fervent lyrics, delightful odes and image-rich narratives, Janlori
Goldman invites us into her world—and it is a deeply moving one. With
fluid, vivid clarity, she valiantly stares at the past, and faces the present with
a compelling mix of temerity and tenderness. Hers is a remarkable voice
that is all at once passionate and exquisitely subtle. One leafs through Gold-
man's book as one would amble through a museum, stopping for a detail
here, an image there, perfectly happy to spend long hours 'in that space, im-
mersed in color and line.'"—Laure-Anne Bosselaar

"Seldom have I seen a book of poems so vital in its storytelling, so rich and
precise in imagery and metaphor, and at the same time so full of heart and
compassion. Like the flocks of starlings Janlori Goldman watches at dusk,
she is herself 'a glimmer sign that all is not lost.'" —Alicia Ostriker

"In this fine book, an intimate, tender voice tells of a life of sensual gladness,
as well as loneliness and grief, most often redeemed by the courage and kindness
of women. The poems most often pay attention to neglected people and neg-
lected truths, often neglected moments, often in the beauty of the earth. Several
among them, 'At the Cubby Hole Bar' and 'Emergency Room,' describe the kind
of holy moments that give us goose flesh."—Jean Valentine

Bread from a Stranger's Oven

Bread from a Stranger's Oven

Janlori Goldman

WHITE PINE PRESS / BUFFALO, NEW YORK

White Pine Press
P.O. Box 236
Buffalo, New York 14201

www.whitepine.org

Acknowledgements:
The Cortland Review, "Grapefruit."
New Millennium Writings, "Still Here" (as "Les Menhirs").
Rattle, "The Story, For Now."
Gwarlingo, "Winter Solstice."
Storyscape Journal, "Chanukah" (as "One Good Turn").
Calyx, "Cyclone" (as "No Matter How Hard").
Contrary, "Yom Kippur," "Elegy for Your Breasts," "Amber Cloud," and "Ode to Stretchmarks."
Mudlark, "The End of the World" and "Washing Dishes in Evergreen, Colorado."
The Sow's Ear, "Elvira" (as "My Neighbor Shot My Cat").
Connotation Press, "That Chocolate Cake," "Sergeant Roy's Reveille," "Burying Ground," "Bungalow, the Catskills," "Bread from a Stranger's Oven," and "Bone Hollow Road."

Anthologies: "At the Cubbyhole Bar," *The American Dream,* Blue Thread Press, 2013.

Publication of this book was made possible, in part, by public funds from the New York State Council on the Arts with the support of Governor Andrew M. Cuomo and the New York State Legislature, a State Agency, and with funds from the National Endowment for the Arts, which believes that a great nation deserves great art.

Cover image: "Fledgling," by Kristin Flynn.

Printed and bound in the United States of America.

ISBN 978-1-945680-06-9

Library of Congress number 2016960877

For my daughter,
Maya Rose Goldman,
and my sweetheart,
Katherine Franke

Contents

I.

Winter Solstice / 15
Washing Dishes in Evergreen, Colorado / 16
Yom Kippur / 18
Bungalow, The Catskills / 19
Summer Flu / 20
Ode to Jacob Blinder / 21
That Chocolate Cake / 22
Burying Ground / 24
Seed Money, 3rd Grade / 25
One Soft Place / 26
Home / 28
Until Mother Put an End to That / 29
Mother, So Happy / 30
Ode To Milton Avery's *Speedboat's Wake*, 1972 / 31

II.

At the Cubbyhole Bar / 35
The End of the World / 37
Amber Cloud / 38
Emergency Room / 39
Elegy for Your Breasts / 40
4 a.m. / 41
The Argument / 42
Cyclone / 43
Elvira / 44
The 8th Circle / 45
Ode to Blue / 46

III.

Bread from a Stranger's Oven / 49
Walking Cure / 50
She-Grief / 51
Cranberries are the Tartest of Fruit / 52
Ode to My Gallbladder / 54
Japanese Beetles / 56
Sergeant Roy's Reveille / 57
Murmuration / 58
Baking in the Last Month / 59
The Waiting Room / 60
The Story, For Now / 61
Two Seeds / 63
Still Here / 64

IV.

Chanukah / 67
The Language of Math / 68
Waiting for Birds / 69
Ode to Stretchmarks / 70
Bone Hollow Road / 72
Tear of the Clouds / 73
Catch What Falls / 74
Magnolia / 75
Knot / 76
Ode to Fever / 77
Blue Blaze / 79
Grapefruit / 80

Notes on the Poems / 81
Tha Author / 82

I bless our hands' daily labor, bless
sleep every night.
Bless night every night.

And the coat, your coat, my coat,
half dust, half holes.
And I bless the peace

in a stranger's house—the bread in a stranger's oven.

—Marina Tsvetaeva

I.

Winter Solstice

Bring me the old season
        that winter familiar

a slow sheathing of moon in shadow
        as if sky were a gill
                through which all things

flow in and filter out—
        bring me a home with no right angles
           a space of curling in

not too bright or sharp
        and bring me the time before that
                with the garden dark with broken-down

coffee grounds and rows of flowering mustard greens
        the smell of ripped roots fresh
                from the pull

and then before that—
        to my round house a friend will come
           or maybe the friend's mother

I'll say, *Stay for dinner*
        she'll say, *Let me sew that button.*

Washing Dishes in Evergreen, Colorado

Bernie holds the chopping knife, tip up, glares at Billie.
      She's asked him to leave the cheese off a burger.
            She put the order in right but the customer,
he changed his mind. Billie's waited on tables
      at The Little Bear since her family stopped ranching, her face
            and hands like smoked snakeskin after years of cigarettes
and wiping counters. By shift's end, the dust of crushed peanut shells
      coats her ankles. Bernie bangs the dishwasher door

            when he finds a greasy plate in the stack. That'd be my fault.
I'm in charge of dishes. I clear tables, haul the clanking mess
      to the back, a quick rinse before loading the aluminum box.
            Unloading is divine—lifting the door at cycle's end, a rush
of wet heat, the smell of ammonia and boil.
      Billie keeps an eye on me so I don't sneak into the bar.
            I eat piles of pepperoni, wait for Bernie to offer a cigarette.
He holds out a pack of Tareyton's.
      I'd rather fight than switch, we say.
            The people in the ads wear a black eye—
proof that a puff is worth a slug.

      The year before, a boy choked me, ripped my heart necklace,
            threw it across the junior high lawn. Mom said, *See?*
You can't be trusted with anything good.
      He was older, jealous of the crush I had on the altar boy
            who sat in front of me in homeroom. I stared at his shiny

black hair, imagined kissing his neck—
      even kneeled in a pew once to see him swing incense.

            Lots of things I wanted were worth getting slugged for.
I almost got punched at the second place I did dishes.
      The register came up short one day.
            I may have taken those twenties

but it's hard to remember what I did
        and what people thought I did.

                The day I lost that job, my mom and her boyfriend
came to the restaurant's side door, said they were driving back
        to New York. The car, packed with her clothes, idled.
                She stood on the steps, said, *Take care of the boys,*
I'll write soon. I picked up a tray of hot glasses
        fresh from the washer. The rack slipped,
                shattered. I can still feel the heat on my palms,

the weight slide from my fingers.
        I was wearing my favorite shirt,
                the one that made me look free—
Indian cotton, tassels at the neck.
        On the street I looked for her blue Skylark.
                By then, they must've made it to the highway.

Yom Kippur

The sunlight didn't break, we are broken,
the word 'broken' is broken.

—Yehuda Amichai

Today everything hurts, and I'm as close to god as I'll ever come
or want to be. I try to forgive myself, fist knocking at my chest,

a door that forgot how to open. The prayer book's spine
against my palms, I sing loudly to drown out the dandruff

flaked on the suit in the next row, sing as if I believe,
as if the fervor had not been rocked out of me by the cantor

whose polioed leg rubbed into me as we sang together in front
of the high holiday congregation, as if I were still his student

and he could still grip my waist—always his smell of yellow breath
and wear. That was when the old men said girls can never be

rabbis, girls can't stand before the torah. And now in the synagogue,
familiar as the couch leg that catches my pinky toe when I walk past it,

I think of the woman asleep in the window well, blonde wisping
out of a hoodie, sneakers on the sidewalk like slippers by a bed.

No, I'm not hungry, she said. I come to this sanctuary from that chill,
wonder if this is the night I'll open the door. If this is the night.

Bungalow, The Catskills

Summer in the woods—my grandparents take only me, leave my brothers.
    Each morning we walk to the neighbor for double-yolked eggs.
        Grandma splits them on the bowl's rim, twin suns
            whisked and scrambled in bacon flecks.
              Eat, shayna maydela, eat.

Chessboard between us, Grandpa teaches me, trust no one: sly knight,
    slanted bishop, aggressive castle, sacrificial pawn.
        You rattle like a teakettle, in Yiddish he says.
            Afternoons, knee-high in the creek rushing with thaw,
              I'm an Iroquois hunter snatching trout.

Rain pummels the tin roof, the barrel overflows, banks days of good flushes,
    even a hairwash. Walnuts fall, still in their shell's shell.
        In Dad's boyhood treasures I find three monkeys
            frozen in jade—*hear no evil, see no evil, speak no evil*—
              roll those chimps in dirty socks,
                smuggle them home.

On the ride back I try not to let it go,
    try to hold the bungalow, the high grass,
        slick river rocks toupée-ed in moss,
            metal cot on the screened porch.

A red fruit turns on a pole,
    the *Big Apple* cafeteria for pie
        and Grandma's lesson in papering the toilet seat—
            her palm on my cheek before sleep.

Summer Flu

Flood me with fever
      bloodboil heat
            that beds me

with wrenched spine
      chatterchill and sweat-
            swings so wild

as to conjure
      a plump hand
            pressed to my forehead

the rough comfort of a worn cloth
      dipped and wrung
            in a cool cistern.

Ode to Jacob Blinder

His face stared out into the living room
       of my grandparents' walk-up on E. 13th.
After they died my father hung him
       on our staircase wall. Bearded and dour,
great-grandfather is now mine, he watches me make coffee,
       scour pans, dance my sweetheart
across the floor.

           Of Jacob Blinder, I know two things:
he never made it out of Russia,
       and of his three daughters,
only the oldest escaped. A constellation of sorrow
       followed her as she lay under hay
in a boxcar across Poland, trailed her
       on the boat to Buenos Aires.

Tell me, Miriam, how did you stow his portrait—
       rolled in your coat hem, a lining in
your satchel, the lost world bound
       to your skirt waist?

           I am named with his 'J'—
though he was surely a Yakov—
       but when the ocean swallowed
a bitter mouthful, it spit back the old language
       at the retreating shore.
When only one thing remains, it isn't hard
       to know what to carry.

That Chocolate Cake

I slip through a hole in the fence,
        go beyond the woods
                to the golf course,

rescue stray balls, pocket the ones
        with busted skin, hours spent prying off
                white armor, unspooling miles

of rubber guts from tight coil
        to limp pile. A country club lady
                invites me to play house,

I am *sweet daughter*, she *kind mother*,
        she bakes me a cake, tawny waves
                of cream, curls of beckoning palm,

sugared tongue. In muddy shoes and jacket bulged
        with balls, I eat my slice,
                she asks about my family,

why I'm not in school. I make stuff up,
        eat another piece. In the woods going home,
                a shock of yellow jackets cut off

my breath. In the swarm, a man—
        he knocks me down, pushes hard,
                grinds my back into roots,

something breaks—
        golf balls fall from pockets,
                endless threads of rubber,

hands of rubber, legs of rubber.
   After the first time, he says,
      it will never hurt again—

the fixed world snaps, no more give.
   Months after the last slice, she calls to me
      in the grocery, the cake lady says my name.

I make a stranger's face. That chocolate cake
   frosted and layered on a glass plate.
      Dirt.

Burying Ground

Forcing the trowel down, I try to remember—
        four inches for hyacinth bulbs,
                tulips deeper for more dark.

And for fat narcissus, *Sir Winston Churchill*
        and *Pheasant's Eye*, how much icy grip
                is needed for bloom?

I rub my knuckles, fret over the coming spring—
        these short days refuse to budge.
                June nights my mother worked her yard,

pruning *American Beauties* and dead-heading
        petunias, the gummy velvet of spent petals
                on her fingers. Tom Seaver

blew her a kiss from the patio tv,
        she watched his twist
                and muscle, prayed

for floodlights and extra innings, for the kids to stay
        asleep. From my room I watched her
                edge the beds, cheer the Mets,

wait until morning to sleep. Here in my yard
        the winter ground yawns as I grip
                the trowel she once held.

Seed Money, 3rd Grade

asters to zinnias
    I sing the list

        bachelor buttons, cosmos, dahlia, forget-me-not, foxglove

anyone home to buy seeds?
    just twenty-five cents a pack

        hollyhocks, johnny jump-ups, morning glory

old ladies answer the bell
    glad for someone at the door

I saved up tips for the swim suit with racing stripes
    and sour sucker candies at the five and dime

dad would kvell   *ah my independent girl*
    you sure can take care of yourself

and how grateful I was for those early jobs
    when dad and mom left us kids to fend

        pansies, petunias, salvia, snap dragons, sweet william

an aluminum bowl under my bed holds coins
    sorted and stacked each week

the smell of metal on my fingers
    the order form a jingle in my head

a lullaby
    yarrow

One Soft Place

You lie at the bottom of the stairs,
        not fallen, just asleep in a nightgown,

at the foot of the stairs in the house
        where you carried three babies.

You don't grudge us so much
        as revile the pounds packed on

by banana cake and ice cream, gulped
        to feed the greedy ones inside—

after each birth, you binge on hardboiled eggs,
        cigarettes, and Sanka. You lock the doors

with us on the outside, run the vacuum at a pitch
        that rankles windows,

bang the broom to drown out the blare of the last
        hit of speed in your palm, that same palm

a mad clockhand Pledge-ing the dining table.
        Such pill-rocketed sheen requires

a do not disturb housekeeping—
        clean sweep polish beat rinse shake.

We chalk the sidewalk, hop squares
        until we can't hold it anymore, bang the door

and press the bell, certain you don't come
        because you don't know we are there,

don't know our need to come in is urgent.
        I see you bend down.

There they are. So immense,
        slow-swinging in the nightgown.

I shouldn't look, but there they are,
        usually bound by choking elastic,

straps that furrow and plowmark your shoulders—
        girdled hosed bleached heeled bolted-down.

I see you at the bottom of the stairs,
        scotched to the gills to shout down the pills,

slogged in the den with the tv still on,
        the emergency test a harsh pitch in the slur.

We step over you to pack lunch for school,
        scour your handbag for change. I want

to burn the ledger, lose the clobbering rage,
        or shove just enough to the side

to make room to crouch down,
        carry you to bed.

Home

In this house of chestnut beams
        one eye on the moon
the other on bluestone
        she waits for death.

Born to this place a breech birth
        she bruised her heels
kicking the door of her mother's tunnel
        tore that woman to oblivion
leaving only yardbirds to raise her
        on grubs and lightning bugs.

She breathes here
        and will die here too
knowing each corner
        and how it fits her
the way light moves
        through the windows
how days tick and seasons shift.

        The house crouches around her
holds her in quilted arms
        until she exhales.

Until Mother Put an End to That

In the refrigerator box with Nancy.
We cut a window with a butter knife,
hang a washcloth curtain, brush and
braid each other's hair, make acorn
gruel. Face to face, knees between
each other's legs, we take turns,
damp smell of cardboard on our
fingers. I want to stay here in this
house, fake-slurp our soup, pull her
to me, ride her bony knee again.

Mother, So Happy

Drunk. She walks into the Atlantic
        swims into that angle
                where wave hits sky.

We three wait on the sand
        like eggs cupped in a carton
                nestled and separate.

Long strokes into swells
        the ocean gulps her
                as she shrinks to mist.

Head and arms in lunar beam
        even her teeth lit
                by a mix of moon and sea.

Disappears as drowned
        only to surface in triumph
                coming up for air.

Full of luck.

Ode to Milton Avery's *Speedboat's Wake*, 1972

The first painting I remember— the day I skipped school,
took the train into the city, hip-huggers and bare feet

up 5th Avenue. In the museum, a zag of white
        painted through marineblue, hours swimming

in the space, immersed in color and line, unmoored
        in a place that made me want to stay afloat,

buoyed on wake, bouyed on wave, in the time before I knew
        how to breathe sky and lie on ocean, before I knew

how much more would be lost. A knotted thread
        tethers me to that canvassed body, Avery's envelope of sea,

where I learn to be the speedboat and its wake,
        the water and the salt that lifts it,

how to carry a stick figure to the end of a line.

II.

At the Cubbyhole Bar

for Donna Bianco, retired sergeant, NYPD

Over two martinis up with olives, you tell me stories
        about your father dead from AIDS, his late-night
fishing pal dead from the same thing.
        Your mother worried she'd caught it.
No, Ma, Pops didn't touch you for twenty years. You're ok.

        Once, after she tried to force you
to eat liver and onions, you threw Barbie and Ken
        down the stairs. As they plunged,
you made them call out, *I'd rather die*
        than eat liver and onions, and your mom
came out of the kitchen crying, tripped over
        the limbs at her feet.

When the planes hit, you were there,
        saved your men, the whole squad,
and they weren't even yours.
        A buddy had asked you to cover his shift
so he could spend the day with his kid.
        You say, *All the guys are getting cancer,*
in the lungs, the stomach, in your case the breasts.

        That morning, after the buildings buckled,
a brown skirt of cloud billowed up.
        You saw her, a bleached blond
in purple satin shirt, no body
        below the waist, thought how a human head
weighs 8 pounds, lifted that weight
        of a newborn, and then the rest. Zipped the bag.

You wanted to be a cop
        because you hated cops,
wanted to be that power.
        At the Canal Street barrier a lady pleaded
to run home, get her dog—
        you said, *No one below Canal*—
but she promised the risk was all on her.
        You knew it didn't work that way,
spoke into her face, *Come back*
        with that dog, bring him this way
 so he can lick my cheek.

The End of the World

Caved and constipated, a bear hibernates
    on muck, hair fused with mud.
        Trees stand iced in sleep,
          relieved of sap.
            Everything rests.

When this world ends, need will evaporate
    in a blink—gone the cycles of knowing,
      going on and not going on,
        fucking and no more, gone
          even the moment when we smell

the obsolescence of breath. The delight
    of apocalypse is that it comes to all
      in the same second—daughters will not be orphans,
        mothers not childless, the fur of life
          merging with frozen ground,

the blossom with its droop.
    We'll go as one, spared
      that gap in mid-air
        when we know
          we're going down.

Amber Cloud

Sleepy heat, all-day drowsing heat,
     like the day I died,
          not for too long

but dead enough for the back
     of a doctor's truck, rolled in a quilt
          from the bed I'd been dreaming in.

     Dying is in me—

the near leap off the 5th floor balcony,
     and the jeep crash, the windshield veined
          by my forehead, the key splitting my knee.

I don't know the difference between *future*
     and *gone*, how to stitch these open nerves,
          ends that never meet.

Bring me a knit cap, make it snug on the scalp.
     Or a pen top to guard the ink
          so I won't spill out.

Emergency Room

A coffee and cookie, a pillow
      under the knees, my father says that all

he needs. He's tired, not from lack of
      sleep, but the other kind

that no amount of rest erases.
      The body is fighting—a skin too thin,

skinny legged, can't shit, fight.
      Still on the gurney, he says,

Remember Akhmatova's egg?
      The one she pressed on Mandelstam

before his first arrest,
      the one meant to be shared

three ways. Here, Anna said. You're going
      to prison. You eat it.

Elegy for Your Breasts

For their heresy, you dress the twin sisters
       in what they deserve, layers

on layers of fabric, drapes hung
       close to the skin,

raiments of unspun wool, burlap,
       damp gabardine—

those heavy, pensive nuns, pendulous
       in full habit, you don't let them

breathe or squint in the sun—
       you want murder by guillotine,

dream of ease in battle
       amazon style

how you'll cock the bow left and right,
       ambidextrous in the field.

4 a.m.

after Henri Michaux

Uprooted hour, sister of lost stars,
        I'm in a sweat—a woman on the other side of life,
in the time when nothing begets nothing.

        Does water move in your country too,
are you awake when the alarm
        rings in a dead language, when night

won't leave, and even goats move
        in the dark, their rusted bells
bleating to the stream.

        We sleep too little—
there's no time—mountains
        block our way.

Who knows one thing to accuse, who knows
        any god? In days ahead
we'll listen to the sway and clank,

        hope not to be noticed.

The Argument

for M.H.

B. walks from room to room

her sister rings the bell

tries her key

but the lock's been changed

she smacks the door

Let me in!

inks a wide slash over the lintel—

a house is safe

until it's not

and then never is again

Cyclone

The twister lifts the home's petticoats,
      holds its skirts
            high over the pasture,

sets a stack of plates in a field.
      Not a teeter or chip,
            just a tidy cylinder of dishes,

pinked with flowers at the rim.
      Where did the cupboard go?
            Now a hay-high expanse

is the breakfront to hold porcelain.
      The house settles down
            on torn roots, a pile of planks

ready with memory
      of how to become a wall.

Elvira

The woman down the road nails it to a tree,
  a sign made from a cardboard box—
    My Neighbor Shot My Cat.

Her rough billboard sells nothing, no
  eggs for sale, fresh-picked corn, pick-up truck
    low miles. No call to arms or action, no *shun*

my murderous neighbor, support
  gun control. The shot cat's owner lives
    in a converted chicken coop,

counts the eggs in her basket,
  hand feeds deer out the back door.
    Hens bookend Elvira on the couch

as they watch a documentary about parrots,
  their heads dip when a hawk screeches
    across the screen. Last Christmas

she cradled her rooster Clark as he died from old age.
  For a time the sign holds up— no
    retractions or updates on the cat's condition,

no p.s. on charges pressed against the junior high boy.
  Through the summer the sign becomes a thing
    on the way, for joggers to run to

and loop back. In heat and rain it wilts—
  My Cat bends into the ground,
    My Neighbor lies under a soggy shutter.

All that's left by fall is *Shot.*

The 8th Circle

Working wet dirt can damage soil.
   I read this today in a gardening handbook,

the kind I rarely crack in my impatience
   to go out with trowel and hoe. But *damage soil?*

What wounds have I dug in, what scabs
   scraped off, forcing the earth

to heal again in perpetual torment, like Dante's
   sowers of discord, slit from *chin*

to farthole, doomed to trudge at the crater's edge
   guts in hand. Once I reveled in rain and muck—

left lovers, abandoned a dog, walked away from a rare
   Chagall poster of newlyweds hovering—

now I wonder how I held a shield against knowing
   what harm I've done in turning

wet ground. How much hurt.

Ode to Blue

I built a blue room, my body.
      Birds fly along the walls, out
      windows and doors. Blue
for this woman who writes a room
      with a poem, no slant meaning
      just true blue sorrow
like the inside of the womb
      I sputtered from,
      seaglass salted
with crossbones and skull,
      stones in my pockets,
      the night's tidal river.
Here I am, suturing the past
      to an hourglassed future,
      sand grains of my pulse
sift to a waiting bed then reverse,
      same grains, new order.
      Blue body of my room,
I lie down in you,
      eyes on bird soar,
      west window.

III.

Bread from a Stranger's Oven

A girl makes her way through forest gems,
      sneakers on a rug of purple violets,

a sequined bandana for her head.
      Under moss she keeps soup cans

and a rusted opener, snacks on early ferns
      and meadow rue.

An oak tracks her height, its low branches
      reach to brush her hair,

crickets and owls up all night tease her to join
      but hers is a solitary game.

She pierces her ears with agates, greases her heels
      in bog, weaves twigs around her waist,

dreams of baking bread, its journey from oven
      to table, where she'll sit,

eyes on the woman's hands holding the loaf,
      the crusted end cupping butter.

Walking Cure

I circle the home turf
      down eighty blocks
            back on a parallel street. No spot

to end up. Shoes spill out
      my closet. I push back
            but they clamber to bust out.

The shoes know—walking
      is the escape hatch
            for trapped breath, a release

from the freeze that lashes me
      to a seat, blurs my view,
            white noise stammer.

Call this *dissociation*: a child
      scrunched under the bed, a dustball
            away from a parent's swiping arm.

A girl on the bed, her training bra
      held against her by the father on top.
            My right hip aches, bone on bone.

I'm wearing down. A chair
      strapped to my back
            wraps its legs around me,

hopes the trek will end
      at a safe place to sit.

She-Grief

Born in the driest season, she comes as dust spiral,
searing dervish, a Fury wailing, until she is that wind,

she is that dust storm, until she raises the gone
from their deadest place, reminds me to attend

to anniversaries of passing, to remember and
remember until I can't swallow, not even water.

Today I'll wash dishes, stare into the postcard's
mountain lake, draw a bergamot bath,

lick the rain from a fig leaf, conjure Karen's cake
made from whole lemons, make my body

a replenishing well. Then when the lost rise up,
I'll quench their parched faces with tears.

Cranberries are the Tartest of Fruit

for my cousin, Dr. Charlotte Silverman, 1913- 2003

Ten eyes on the ends of your toes
    watch me lift your feet
        into a pink plastic tub.

Now hundreds of sudsy eyes blink
    as I scoop warm water around
        your ankles, up your calves.

Like the first time I bathed my daughter.
    Her slippery skin cringed in the air
        as I bent over the kitchen sink,

sank her downy shoulders in faux amnio—
    wondered how many newborns
        slip to linoleum, how many

mothers swab the floor of evidence.
    Your feet, heavier than a whole baby
        and with nowhere to fall,

shed scales laid-in during that immobile
    spring. A blue washcloth
        coaxes off another layer.

Stainless steel clippers and scissors
    of every kind fill a jar in the cabinet,
        a precise array to slip

under sutures, slice skin, snip
    surgical thread, clip toenails.
        My hands anchor your ankles

in a slop of dinosaur nails.
    You instruct me, the surgeon
        guiding her rookie nurse.

Ode to my Gallbladder

Lazy sac, you lay about always late for the job
    and what an easy job it is,
all you need to do is notice when I eat,
    that's your cue to show up,
spray that voodoo juice you're hoarding,
    let go a few squirts of your secret cocktail,
make it go down real easy—
    where are you? worn out or hung over,
trying to get my attention?
    Well wake up, maybe after half a century
you're walking off the set,
    taking early retirement, leaving me—
sure, I've been left before,
    but hey little guy, let's make up,
I'm attached to you, snug up under
    my ribs, I've shielded you
from heartache and desk jobs,
    all I asked in return was for you to
ice the cake as it passed by, to let fly
    some of your triple-X sauce on the tamale,
and when nothing came your way,
    you were off the clock, free to boogie
with the liver all night long.
    You should be grateful you're not heart
or lungs working 24/7 with no overtime.
    Aha, I see it now,
I've given you too much leash,
    flex-time broke your work ethic—
O most tiny organ,
    unruly mollusk, you were begging for limits,
crying out for schoolhouse walls

and I ignored you.
Greedy lout, hold your bile.
     Live out your measly days
all jammed up in scrabble and grit.
     I can live without you,
really I can. You leave me
     no choice.

Japanese Beetles

His pant legs empty, a man on a skateboard
        shakes a coffee can,

offers a tiny American flag.
        Why doesn't he tie up

the hollow cloth, tuck it under?
        For a small coin I can look longer

at his missing legs—I ask Grandpa for a dime.
        He grabs the flag. *See?*

Made in Japan. Japs with their bombs
        and tricks. This guy's a faker, walks just fine.

Fifty years later, when bugs chew my rose buds,
        mangle June bloom, I mix water

and dish soap in a rusted can, flick
        the insects to drown in slippery bubbles.

Sergeant Roy's Reveille

Neighbors grumble under their quilts
        but nothing and nobody stops you—
at 7:30 every morning you mow,

ride around and around your yard.
        I see you peek between fence slats,
tangled white hair unshorn since the war,

hoping to provoke a complaint.
        I grit and grimace, knowing
that at the last path of crew-cut grass,

after circling the '65 Chevy Nova,
        past the boat on blocks
and glider stilled in vines and rust—

the engine chokes to a halt.
        You are one of those men, Roy,
there are so many of you.

I am tired of living
        in your battle.
This morning, let's sleep in.

Murmuration

Watch these birds as light sifts
through April's dusk, flocks of thousands careen
into a single being,

see how they swing, a magician's cloak
stitched of starlings, inky velvet swooping down,
lifting up over the canyon's ridge.

I thought murmuration was sound
but now I realize it's something else
and the word is beyond what we can hear—

it's spirit-ash hovering over river,
a mumble of moans in the air, goosebumped nights
turned and tossed, flecks of regret troubling the lines.

Two strangers kettling up to taste the wind,
the split self coming together.
A glimmer sign that all is not lost.

Baking in the Last Month

Rosemary-soaked olives and sea salt. My mouth
      in licked delirium from this warm bread.

Yeast swells, opens the well of *yearn* and *ache,*
      the grain at its start. Darkening under the eyes,

a darker line from the navel straight down, this rise
      a sign of life inside, my acre swollen to the brim.

In a shallow pool I lie cooling, a slow fish
      carrying a slower fish, who flips

like a caught trout, rolls a fin against her cell.
      In July my girl makes a fist, crowns in a streak

of rouge. I want to see the time ahead,
      of well-springs and *be good*—we do

have to be good. Unclamp the breath,
      knot the cord. My small deed.

The Waiting Room

I watch the river eddy north
    and south in jumbled currents.
        What grabs on pulls away. What pulls away
           finds a spot to spin,
              in its wake the memory of leaving.

Let me tell you about sound—
    yes, it is this slip of sea
        sheltered from open water,
           and language as it splits
              from the body, a word with a cry at its center,

and yes, sound is an unmuddled mind,
    or to do deeply like sleep, swaddled
        in first blanket, unable
           to fly away.

And the sound of *no sleep?*
    me rocking next to my newborn in intensive care,
        the ricochet of a heart monitor's beeps against her plastic cocoon,
           the hee and haw of a doctor's voice, that same donkey who
              delivered my baby blue, who said,
                Don't get your hopes up.

Momma, leave on the light.
    I don't want to be alone. I'm afraid
        when I scream
        no one will hear.

Come home, baby girl.
    That doctor doesn't know
        how we survive.

The Story, For Now

No father. That's what I told you.
    By second grade friends said,
        All kids have one, somewhere,

they called you *liar.* And the difference between *biology*
    and *Dad?* That's the story that grew
        as you grew, like dated pencil marks

on the doorframe. Now I tell you—
    I met him on a work trip.
        In the morning, we circled Henry Moore's

massive, marble women. *A divorce,*
    he said he was getting one. I said,
        You should know, I'm going to have

this baby, I'm not asking you for anything,
    I knew nothing of asking.
        To the mound under my sweater, he said,

You can always make another. This one
    will ruin my life. The wife and I,
        we're working things out.

I agreed to keep his secret,
    on your birth certificate wrote
        No Father, just xxxxxxxxx.

When you were young I told you,
    A friend helped me, a woman
        needs sperm to make a baby—

this is true the way a story with missing lines
        can be true. By twelve you ask,
                What was your friend's name?

I forgot, I say. You hear the lie,
        demand I put his picture and name
                in the piano bench, inside the purple book

with mirrors on the cover. *Is he good at math?*
        Do I have a brother?
                He should've wanted to know me,

should've told his wife—aren't you angry?
        I thought I'd given you enough of a story,
                but under the clapboard a vine's been growing,

a prying wedge. I tell you now, I am angry.
        For not knowing you'd long to fill in the blank
                with something other than a string of x's.

Two Seeds

She holds the book up to her chest,
      compares her bird's eye
nipples to the pictured stages—
      breast buds, Momma.

It's a long way from conception
      to here, the phone call to him,
a kicked-door broken toe,
      cat dying under the bed.

All those redemption movies,
      you know, where the nearly dead
father says sorry, begs absolution,
      screen fills with blurred hugs,

last breath. That's why this grown child,
      with her own child growing
holds out for that scene, full of dumb hope
      and the memory of fruit—

how a thing looks in its bud phase,
      before you realize you're still sitting
in the theater, the screen's gone dark,
      a broom scratching at popcorn bits.

Still Here

A river begins
at the top of a mountain, from rainfall
or spring, gathers mass and speed,

quenches a dusty bone, wets a meadow,
turns sheep to drier pasture.
We come from this,

seasons of trickle and rush, flood
and parch—the lucky break into the sea.
It is hard to see bruises on water.

If we can just reach ocean, even harbor
or lake, our only duty will be to heal.
Confide to fish, if they'll listen,

to snails, if they can hear.
We gather containers to hold us for a bit, until
the next bend—like a bowl carved

before the harvest, a quilt sewn
though there's no new life to swaddle.
Standing over that water,

on a spot less bridge than plank,
the call comes from the deep, *We'll make*
a way, come back.

IV.

Chanukah

My girl and I buy potatoes,
make latkes, light the menorah,

and tell the story of a miracle,
our own miracle of the one who

disappeared from the sonogram.
A miscarriage, said the doctor,

but I said, *No, my baby will find
a way out*—days later he looked again.

There, a spark, clinging to her sac.

The Language of Math

for Maya Rose

In pink sneakers circling up the stairs, you turn
    to check on me—out of breath, gripping the rail—
        your eyerolls sweeter than other days when my dumbness

can be astounding. These 14 years I've learned how to get you to *blue*
    by saying *red*, to explain the difference between *daddy*
        and *sperm*. Curled into a desk on parents' night,

I hear what you hear each day: *roots in common,*
    cross multiply, raise it to the nth power—
        I look out on the Hudson, gaze north in Spanish,

south in physics— dredgers, tourist boats, helicoptering gulls.
    You learn: *two points determine a segment,*
        all segments have one midpoint.

Teach me that intersecting space where things make sense,
    where we can find each other. I want to know
        Fibonacci's Sequence in bee mating,

seeds in a sunflower, the pinecone's spikes.
    Teach me numbers, the power to push,
        or not to push at all.

Waiting for Birds

When my daughter left for college
      I ran away from home

to a place of no schedules
      no school day

no cool palm to lay on her forehead
      to check for fever

no walking by the still room
      a worn sock under the bed.

I come to a place to sit
      watch fishing boats putter the coastline

lights cluster on the sea at 4 a.m.—
      that used to be the hour

of no crying and no lost shoe
      of pages turned and lights out—

this day I wake in dark
      a thin grip on the hour.

Ode to Stretchmarks

You silver spiders, skinny legs criss-crossing
        my hips, sneaky thief of taut and allure,
                how you snakedance on my belly

like seaweed swaying in the brine,
        waving a sign—used womb,
                empty lot—you made your move, a hostile

takeover, some kind of adverse
        possession, multiplying like mice
                in the pantry's warm nook, blind

newborns nuzzling in nests of castoff hair,
        nosing around for a lick of pastry flour
                or macaroni nibble, a universe

of spindled creatures making me
        their center, incubating in the belly's button,
                site of the shorn umbilicus useful again.

You are like that, colonizers with intricate bridges
        and sideroads, a Baghdad café
                for all the poets to come shake it

and sweat, you're a houseparty on hips,
        iridescent when lights blow out,
                enough milky moon to shimmy by.

Teacher of this stubborn child,
        why did I ever fight you?
                Icing on my cake,

you life's proof,
     I join the party—
          welcome to my body.

Bone Hollow Road

The moon's in heat, chiffoned in crimson gauze.
       In the meadow deer eat apples, nibble from trees

they trust are meant for them.
       The day before fruit is perfect to pick,

they stand at low branches for easy bites,
       lift high on hoof-tip for the greedy getting—

give me Romes, Cortlands, Macouns.
       Now begins the season of deer under apples,

 red moon low, raccoon young without mother,
       and addled postmistress confused by scale,

who ponders how much it'll cost
       to get a small package out of here.

Tear of the Clouds

Hudson, you begin as a trickle
       from an Adirondack lake.
            Tell me, are you born

from a rip in the cumulous
       or a drop of regret from the sky?
            Maybe sorrow needs a gash in the atmosphere

to rain down, join all the other sorry run-offs
       and rills on their way to you,
            so delirious with weeping

you flow both ways. Big Bawling River,
       you're a serpent of unsure mind, salty downstream
            but up north your water's sweet.

Happiest when submerged, I could be one leg over
       or torso between the bars.
            An aluminum rail warns,

stay on land. The metal repeats,
       go wash dishes, take a bath.

Catch What Falls

for Katherine

In heavy coat and dark scarves you arrive,
  eyes startled from across an ocean.

Come, lay down those bundles,
  let me take your damp sweater,

wrap your shoulders in shawl.
  Let's watch the sky for Bellatrix's spark,

our amazon star—the constellation's
  mighty tongue, your waiting mouth.

Magnolia

Young sap, dwarfed and rootcramped,
    you twine your limbs to shield a bare torso,
        mortified most in bud days when scant tips

of pea fingers are all you push out.
    Did you want to go with her ex- to Holland, crated
        with a slat-worn bench and Dutch cookbooks? Timid sprig, less

cherished than a clay pot or last slip of soap at the sink.
    Well, there was no tussle for you, not even a thumb wrestle.
        All that misery shoveled over you, no wonder you're pale.

I came later as the next and last sweetheart
    of the one who stayed, offered a move to a breezier spot,
        a loamy cloak streaked with worms. Even so, I'm no saint:

a tirade at Dutchgirl's photo in the bedside drawer,
    a hurl of the red nail polish left in the cabinet. All to the trash.
        But not you, Magnolia, you're mine now.

Our first winter you gathered steam beneath an icy wreath
    as my new love and I wept, heaved decades of dirt,
        cracked the soil to receive the March soak.

Knot

A small brown bird flies into my hair,
        at first to nest there,

but soon it's trapped—
        flaps, barely churns wind,

weaves long strands
        through its wings.

A snarled ball
        at my nape,

it chafes to escape,
        pecks my scalp

with that beak
        built to crack nuts—

quite a pair we make,
        hardhead and seedbuster.

Ode to Fever

You tentacled fire
        pitch of desire
you spine dissolving rampage
        a wordmangler in my bed
purveryor of drenched dreams
        your wave is all tumult and toss—
once you brought a cool cloth
        to that cot in grandma's bungalow
her hands lay an ice-soaked rag
        across my forehead
she scolded you with shoo-shoo
        rummaged in her trick bag for the hex
that would chase your troubled ass
        down the road and into the creek
snare you in its chilly grip—
        yes she carried magic
that voodoo love that rescued me
        from a flaming end
saved me from disgracing the myth
        of a child's immunity
gave me a shield against a wily heat
        stomping through my blood
with invaders' hooves
        a spirit hot with vengeance
intent on making me sweat
        making me hallucinate an ice block
a walk-in freezer
        a lay-me-down
in redemption's frozen lake
        how the water pops and sizzles
how it holds me in forgiving arms

its witch's fingers on my eyelids
my nape and thirsty throat
            under shoulderblades on wrists
and between thighs
            where my waiting vee hollers
touch me there Bruja
            bring this heat to its knees
breathe your arctic breath
            into my tangled hair singed and smoky
now that would be some true kindness—O Fever
            look how you try to melt me
look how you refuse to go.

Blue Blaze

For my birthday my sweetheart gave me a '91 Ford pickup,
        rusted and driven hard.

I climb in, sit up high. A mix of wet dog, motor oil,
        and adolescent armpit reminds me I'm not the first.

Dunkin' Donuts napkins and greasy pens jam the glove box.
        I learned to drive on my boyfriend's truck, *Phred,*

a stick so cranky each shift demanded a shove.
        And that scratchy front seat, built like a cot.

In my new hauler with its smooth ride,
        I'm glad to be 49, glad to be

shoveling a load of wet mulch out the back,
        working it into a pile next to the wood stack.

Bring on sleet and chill. We've enough
        to keep the stove stoked.

Grapefruit

When I eat a grapefruit I peel the whole thing,
      thumb-open pink sections, let slick liquid drip from chin
to table, a sticky scene of mayhem and grin.
      Maybe there's a plate or napkin but grapefruit doesn't care
for being contained, sprays like a hot day's sprinkler
      on a running child, like the first uncorked pour of bubbly
foaming over the rim—or the Hudson in a hurricane,
      how it waves its finger, rises up on streets, traps a man
waiting out his shift. And there, in that parking garage,
      the river finds its lowest point, one man from Ghana
who vowed to bring his family across the ocean.
      Into that gape water rises fast, slams a door.
Though a rescue team blows up a raft and paddles down the street,
      though black caps with flashlights dock
and try to enter, though they call and call, they hear water,
      only water, see the maw guzzling its fill,
gulping river as the whale took its Jonah.
      They retreat, drift back to dry land
until the next day when the Hudson returns to its banks,
      neither sheepish nor repentant, just drained
of tantrum. Then Anthony Narh is delivered, lifted out
      with swollen cars. Flower bunches lean
on the shuttered space, the space I see as grapefruit
      bursts its skin, makes such sticky innocent mess,
ritual morning mess, as I watch the street,
      keep an eye on that river.

Notes on the Poems

The epigraph is a Marina Tsvetaeva poem, translated by Ilya Kaminsky and Jean Valentine in *Dark Elderberry Branch*, Alice James Books, 2012.

"Grapefruit" is dedicated to Gerald Stern.

"Amber Cloud" comes from an essay by the late Professor Derrick Bell, published in *And We Are Not Saved: The Elusive Quest for Racial Justice.* New York: Basic Books. 1989. Bell's "cloud" is a fabled affliction, dubbed "ghetto disease," that darkens the skin of privileged white kids, and makes them "lethargic, suspicious, withdrawn, and hopelessly insecure."

Janlori Goldman is a poet, teacher and activist. *Bread from a Stranger's Oven* is her first full-length book. Her chapbook, *Akhmatova's Egg*, was published by Toadlily Press. Gerald Stern chose her poem "At the Cubbyhole Bar" for the 2012 Raynes Prize. Janlori's poetry has been widely published, including in *The Cortland Review, Mead, Gwarlingo, Connotation Press, Calyx, Gertrude, Mudlark, The Sow's Ear, Rattle,* and *Contrary*. She co-founded *The Wide Shore: A Journal of Global Women's Poetry*, www.thewideshore.org. She worked with Paris Press on the joint publication of Virginia Woolf's essay "On Being Ill" with Ms. Woolf's mother, Julia Stephen's, guide to nursing, "Notes from Sick Rooms."

For nearly twenty years, Janlori was a civil rights lawyer in Washington D.C. She is a professor of human rights and public health and volunteers as a writing mentor at Memorial Sloan Kettering Cancer Center. She received an MFA from Sarah Lawrence College.

With Gratitude—

For good and generous teachers: especially Laure-Anne Bosselaar, Ellen Bryant Voigt, David Groff, Suzanne Hoover, Ilya Kaminsky, Joan Larkin, Dennis Nurkse, Victoria Redel, Martha Rhodes, Brenda Shaughnessy, Jean Valentine, and in memory, Tom Lux and Rachel Wetzsteon. To Susan Guma and Sarah Lawrence College, who let me slip in under the fence to be a student again.

For the love of my daughter, Maya Rose, and my brothers, Michael and David, who barely flinched at these poems. And for the love of my sisters, Karen, D2, and Jane. For the stunning women who shared poems in the 'O' room—Zdena, Monica, Laura, Lee, Victoria—and friends who believed that poetry could save me, especially Susan Biegler, Florrie Burke, Penny Damaskos, Hope Gleicher, Julie Goldscheid, Barbara Hammer, Carla Kjellberg, Jane Larson, Linda Longmire, Sandy Mullin, and Rachel Simon. And for first readers Lorraine Healy, Monica Hand and Jake Berthot.

And for my *first* first reader Katherine, fierce and full of joy.

THE WHITE PINE PRESS POETRY PRIZE

Vol. 22   *Bread From a Stranger's Oven* by Janlori Goldman. Selected by Laure-Anne Bosselaar.

Vol. 21   *The Brighter House* by Kim Garcia. Selected by Jericho Brown.

Vol. 20   *Some Girls* by Janet McNally. Selected by Ellen Bass.

Vol. 19   *Risk* by Tim Skeen. Selected by Gary Young.

Vol. 18   *What Euclid's Third Axiom Neglects to Mention About Circles* by Carolyn Moore. Selected by Patricia Spears Jones.

Vol. 17   *Notes from the Journey Westward* by Joe Wilkins. Selected by Samuel Green.

Vol. 16   *Still Life* by Alexander Long. Selected by Aliki Barnstone.

Vol. 15   *Letters From the Emily Dickinson Room* by Kelli Russell Agodon. Selected by Carl Dennis.

Vol. 14   *In Advance of All Parting* by Ansie Baird. Selected by Roo Borson.

Vol. 13   *Ghost Alphabet* by Al Maginnes. Selected by Peter Johnson.

Vol. 12   *Paper Pavilion* by Jennifer Kwon Dobbs. Selected by Genie Zeiger.

Vol. 11   *The Trouble with a Short Horse in Montana* by Roy Bentley. Selected by John Brandi.

Vol. 10   *The Precarious Rhetoric of Angels* by George Looney. Selected by Nin Andrews.

Vol. 9   *The Burning Point* by Frances Richey. Selected by Stephen Corey.

Vol. 8   *Watching Cartoons Before Attending A Funeral* by John Surowiecki. Selected by C.D. Wright.

Vol. 7   *My Father Sings, To My Embarrassment* by Sandra Castillo.
         Selected by Cornelius Eady.

Vol. 6   *If Not For These Wrinkles of Darkness* by Stephen Frech.
         Selected by Pattiann Rogers.

Vol. 5   *Trouble in History* by David Keller. Selected by Pablo Medina.

Vol. 4   *Winged Insects* by Joel Long. Selected by Jane Hirshfield.

Vol. 3   *A Gathering of Mother Tongues* by Jacqueline Joan Johnson.
         Selected by Maurice Kenny.

Vol. 2   *Bodily Course* by Deborah Gorlin. Selected by Mekeel McBride.

Vol. 1   *Zoo & Cathedral* by Nancy Johnson. Selected by David St. John.